CONTENTS

The Nightmare Begins...   2

Chapter 1   4

Chapter 2   12

Chapter 3   16

Chapter 4   20

Chapter 5   25

THE NIGHTMARE BEGINS...

This morning, I was a normal kid. But by the end of the day, I'd become a hunted animal. And it was all because of Cindy Mackle.

The nightmare started on the way home from school. Of course, at the time, I didn't know it was the start of a nightmare. If I had, I would have gotten away from Cindy as fast as I could. But when someone asks you an ordinary question, you don't expect it to turn into a horror story or a nightmare – like when you're dreaming that you are running from a pride of lions, and your feet stick in the mud, and the lions are getting closer and closer. What happened today was just like that. It makes me shiver even thinking about it.

CHAPTER 1

I am walking home with Mungo and Scott, as usual. We are discussing things to do at our club when Cindy Mackle catches up with us.

Scott wiggles his eyebrows at Mungo and me. That's our secret sign to stop talking about the club. Then comes the question that starts the nightmare.

"Can I belong to your club?" Cindy Mackle asks.

The three of us sound like startled chickens.

"What club?"

"Whose club?"

"Huh!" (Mungo always says "Huh!" when he can't think of what to say.)

We all look at Cindy in horror, but she just puts her hands on her hips and laughs at us.

"You know! The club you have in the old garden shed in your backyard," says Cindy, turning her big brown eyes toward me.

I try to think of something to get her off track. "That old shed? We've been cleaning it out."

"Yeah," adds Scott.

"What, after dark with flashlights?"

Cindy is smart and likes a laugh. She moved into the neighborhood two weeks ago, and she already knows most of what's happening and what's already happened. She lives on the next street, but our yards back into each other, with an old wooden fence between. She has the longest black hair I've ever seen. On her second day at school, she wore it down. It came to her waist. She told the class she'd never had it cut. Totally amazing.

It looked like a sheet of shiny black plastic.

"So...?" Cindy stares hard at us.

"Hang on," I say. "There are rules and things..."

"That's right! Rules!" adds Scott.

"Yeah! Rules!" echoes Mungo.

"What sort of rules?"

Mungo and Scott stare at me in total silence. We are left without a leg to stand on. We don't have any rules for the club. Not one.

"Don't take too long deciding about your rules," Cindy says with a little smile on her face. "Otherwise, I might have to tell Mr. Jenkins where his old rope is."

"We've only borrowed..."

"Quiet, Scott!" I whisper.

Mr. Jenkins lives at the end of the street, and his house is next to Scott's.

We borrowed his old rope for a swing bridge between the two trees behind our clubhouse, but it didn't work. Now the rope is lying, like a dead snake, in the grass.

We move away from Cindy and start whispering.

"We can't let her join."

"But she knows about the rope."

"All we need is one rule. Something that would definitely stop her from being able to join."

"What's the problem?" teases Cindy. "Forgotten the rules?"

"She knows we don't have any rules," says Scott desperately.

Then, just when everything is looking totally hopeless, Mungo comes up with a brilliant idea.

"How about," Mungo says, "you can't join unless you have short hair."

I told you it was a brilliant idea. It couldn't fail. There was no way Cindy would have her hair cut just so she could join our club. Sometimes Mungo has some stupid ideas, but this time... Wow!

"You tell her," he says to me.

We turn around and face Cindy.

"The first rule is that you have to have short hair."

"Short, short hair," adds Mungo, going a little overboard with his brilliant idea.

I expect Cindy to tell us it's not fair. Then I'll tell her that the second rule is that no rules are allowed to be broken.

"OK," she says.

"But... but you have long hair," I whimper.

Mungo and Scott look at me with pale faces.

"So... I'll get it cut."

"Short, short," says Mungo.

"What about your mother?" I ask.

Something is happening. Mungo's brilliant plan is going belly-up.

"It's *my* hair," says Cindy.

I don't know what to say. Is she putting us on? Is she seeing how far she can string us along? She must be. I decide to play her game. "OK. Get it cut and you can join our club!"

"What?" exclaims Scott.

"Huh!"

"Don't worry," I whisper out of the side of my mouth. "She'll chicken out. You watch."

The next moment is the most awful one in my entire life. Cindy doesn't chicken out. Instead she says, "Which one of you is going to cut it?"

CHAPTER 2

Looking back now, I can see what Cindy was up to. She was waiting for us to chicken out. That was when I should have left. I should have walked away and gone home to mow the grass or wash the dishes without being asked – even if it got Mom worried about me. Anything but hang around. But like a nightmare, once you're in it, it's hard to get out.

"You could draw straws to see who is going to be the lucky person to cut my hair," suggests Cindy.

The *lucky* person? I still can't believe she's actually going to go through with it, especially just to join our club! All we do is hang out in an old shed.

The three of us stand, like cardboard cutouts, with open mouths.

Then Scott springs to life. "We don't have any straws," he says.

"We could use pieces of paper," suggests Mungo. Sometimes, I wonder whose side he's on.

Before Scott and I can protest, Cindy rips a page out of her notebook. Then she tears the page into three different lengths.

"Close your eyes!" she orders.

When we open our eyes, the pieces of ripped paper are sticking out from her clenched hand. They all look the same size.

"The person who pulls the shortest one gets to cut my hair."

None of us protest. It's as if we're totally powerless.

"Who wants to go first?" asks Cindy with a grin.

"Mungo does," Scott and I say together.

"Huh!"

"Take one!" says Cindy. She holds out her hand. Mungo nervously shuffles his feet.

"Hurry up!" I yell. All of this is starting to get on my nerves.

Mungo pulls out a long strip. He grins with relief.

"Next!" says Cindy.

Scott takes one. He pulls it out slowly, then waves it in my face. It's a long one as well.

Cindy uncurls her fingers. Lying in her palm is the last strip of paper. It is very short. And there is no doubt at all who the lucky one is – the one who is going to get to cut Cindy Mackle's long black hair.

CHAPTER 3

Before I can make an excuse, I find myself being herded down the street by Cindy.

"Now," she says. "You can cut my hair while my mom's out."

I clear my throat. "But don't you like having long hair?" I know I sound like a wimp, but that's too bad. There's no way I want to be the one to cut Cindy's hair.

Cindy just laughs. "It's too heavy, and it takes hours to dry after I wash it. I'm sick of it."

I'm not sure when Mungo and Scott actually disappear, but one minute they're behind us, and the next, they are completely out of sight.

This is when I decide to make up rule number three: In times of emergency, we stick together. No matter what! Deserters are expelled from the club.

"You're not scared, are you?" says Cindy, leading me around to the back door of her house.

I shake my head. "No problem."

Before going into Cindy's house, I turn and look over the fence at our clothes line. I can see my mom's blue jeans, two of my T-shirts, and a whole lot of my little sister's clothes. At that moment, I'd give anything to be on the other side of the fence.

"Come on!" says Cindy.

I trail into the kitchen behind her. After dumping her backpack on the kitchen table, Cindy goes to the cupboard and takes out a loaf of bread. "Want some?"

"Not hungry," I lie. How can she think of eating at a time like this?

I take off my backpack and wait. I keep hoping she'll tell me it's a joke.

Maybe she'll say she's been putting me on. Instead, she carefully butters the two slices of bread then spreads on a thick layer of peanut butter. She eats them very slowly.

When she's finished, she leaves and comes back with a pair of scissors. The long blades make a swishing sound as she opens and closes them.

CHAPTER 4

"Now remember – short. Real short," says Cindy, sitting herself down in a chair. If only Mungo hadn't added on the extra part about her hair having to be real short, I might have been able to get away without cutting too much. Mungo the Bungo!

Even as Cindy undoes her hair and lets it spread over her back, like the night sky, and even as she hands me the scissors, I'm still waiting for her to shout, "Got you!" But she doesn't.

I take a handful of her hair and crunch into it with the scissors, and the nightmare hits me full force. It's worse than dreaming about a pride of angry lions, and mountains of mud, and stuck feet. I just want to wake up, but I can't wake up. I'm not asleep.

I cannot believe this is really happening. I'm really cutting Cindy Mackle's long hair.

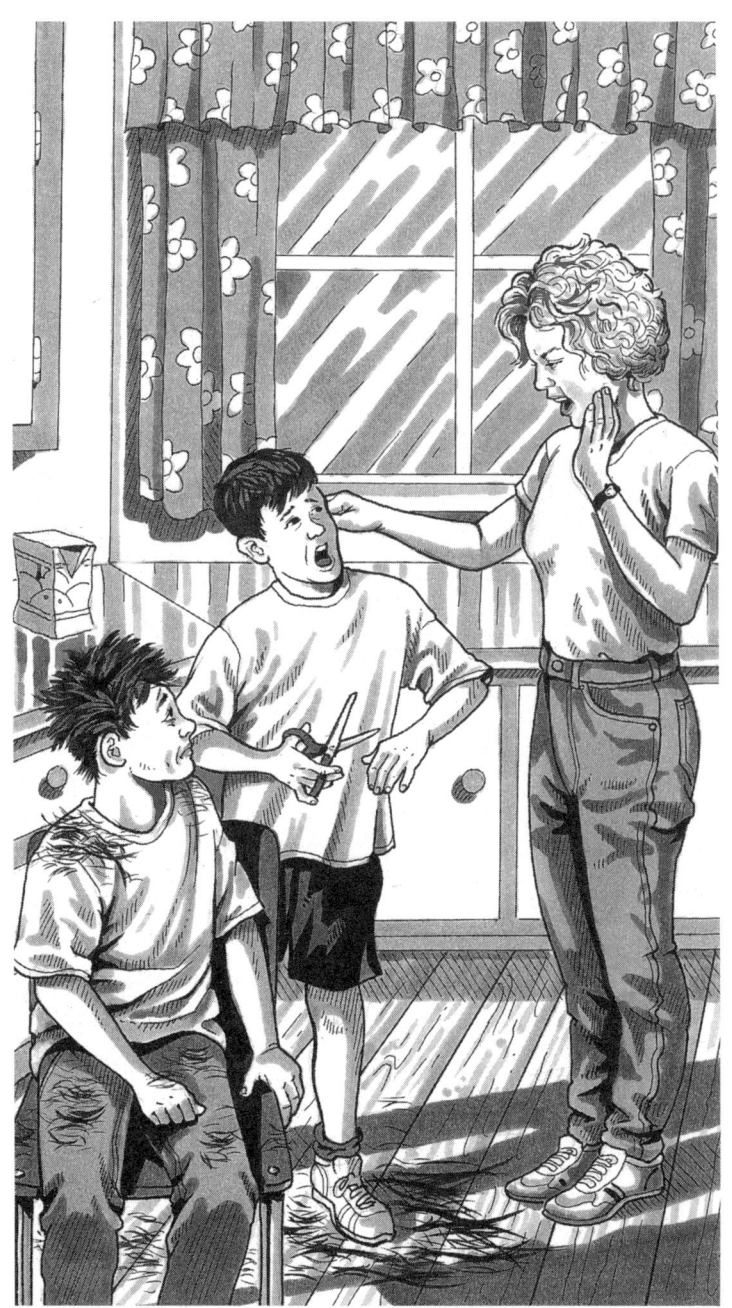

In minutes, most of Cindy's hair lies on the floor. It's like a deep, black puddle around my feet.

"What's it look like?" asks Cindy.

I gaze at her head. The hair that is left erupts in spikes and stalks.

Then, before I can reply, Mrs. Mackle opens the kitchen door.

After that, I don't know what happens. Someone screams. At first, I think it's me, but then I realize it's her. The scream is so awful, I nearly faint with fright.

CHAPTER 5

I don't know how I got out of Cindy Mackle's house alive.

By the time I arrive home, Mom is waiting for me. The nightmare is filling up with more and more horrible people. Usually, Mom is nice. Usually, she smiles a lot and teases me. Usually... But today she starts yelling at me before I'm halfway in the house.

"What on earth possessed you..." After the first minute, I block out her words. Instead, I wonder what it would be like to be a uvula, stuck at the back of a throat – day after day after day – just hanging around. Except for times like this, when a uvula gets to do a lot of waving, I've never seen one so close before.

Now, thirty minutes later, I am shut up in my bedroom, just like a caged animal. No dinner! No TV! And wouldn't you know it, Wednesday night is the best TV night of the week! Mom told me to think about what I've done. I have, over and over. And I still think there was no way out. I still think it was Cindy's fault. I wish I'd never heard of her. I wish we never had a club...

A knock on my door interrupts my sad thoughts. I suppose it's time for another long lecture. But it isn't Mom. It's Cindy.

"It's OK," she says. "I told my mom that I made you cut my hair."

"Really?"

She nods. "Anyway, I did, didn't I?"

I don't argue. The smell of bacon and potatoes cooking in the kitchen is driving me crazy. I need to eat! Then I laugh. Cindy's hair looks like it's been chewed. Worse than that! It looks like it's been cut with an old, rusty lawnmower.

Cindy grins. "There was no way my mom was ever going to let me get it cut," she says. "Now she can't do anything about it. Thanks, Amos."

I shrug.

"So, do we have a deal?"

A deal? What's she talking about?

"You know, that I can join your club," Cindy says.

I hesitate, then spit into my palm. Cindy does the same.

"OK. It's a deal," I say. We smack our hands together.

While I'm watching my favorite TV show, it dawns on me that I haven't told Scott and Mungo the good news about our newest club member. That's too bad. There's absolutely no way I want to have two nightmares in the same day. One is more than enough! The next one will have to wait until tomorrow!

FROM THE AUTHOR

When we were children, my half-brother (I'll call him Timothy to protect his identity) always played with a little friend from down the road. One day, they found my mother's dressmaking scissors and decided to play "hairdresser." Timothy proceeded to cut off his friend's hair and then, as if this was not enough, he painted her skull with some old red paint he found in the garage. That was when the nightmare began – not only for Timothy, but for our mother, too.

Elizabeth Pulford

FROM THE ILLUSTRATOR

When I finished school, I pursued my childhood ambition to work as an artist. In my first job, at a surplus supply store, I drew hundreds of illustrations of clothing and boots. From there, I went on to illustrating comic strips and creating T-shirt designs. Today, I am doing what I love best: illustrating children's books. Sometimes, however, books present artists with nightmares, too. What would you do, as an illustrator, with a braided ponytail, a boy, a pair of scissors, and an empty cover page?

Richard Hoit

FRIENDS AND FRIENDSHIP
Uncle Tease
PS I Love You, Gramps
Friendship in Action
Midnight Rescue
Nightmare
You Can Canoe!

ACTION AND ADVENTURE
Dinosaur Girl
Amelia Earhart
Taking to the Air
No Trouble at All!
River Runners
The Midnight Pig

WILD AND WONDERFUL
Winter Survival
Peter the Pumpkin-Eater
Because of Walter
Humphrey
Hairy Little Critters
The Story of Small Fry

ALL THE WORLD'S A STAGE
All the World's a Stage!
Which Way, Jack?
The Bad Luck of King Fred
Famous Animals
Puppets
The Wish Fish

Written by **Elizabeth Pulford**
Illustrated by **Richard Hoit**
Edited by **Sue Ledington**
Designed by **Kristie Rogers**

© 1997 Shortland Publications Inc.
All rights reserved.

04 03 02 01 00
10 9 8 7 6 5 4 3

Distributed in the United States of America by
  Rigby
  a division of Reed Elsevier Inc.
  P.O. Box 797
  Crystal Lake, IL 60039-0797

Printed by Colorcraft, Hong Kong
ISBN: 0-7901-1650-2